Legendary Creatures

Tamim Ansary

Illustrations by Derrick Williams

1 2 3 4 5 6 7 8 9 10
ISBN 0-8250-4969-X

Walch Publishing
P. O. Box 658 • Portland, Maine 04104-0658
walch.com

Printed in the United States of America

Table of Contents

Introduction

Once upon a time the world was filled with legendary creatures. That's because no one had seen much of the world yet. No one knew what to think when a hunter came home with some strange story. He might have told everyone he had seen a beast bigger than 100 men. He might have added that it had two teeth like curved spears. What if he said its nose was like a vine? People might call this beast unbelievable. But today we would call such a beast an elephant.

Over time, many strange beasts have been caught and studied. We have given them names. We have learned the truth behind the stories. But some unbelievable beasts have never been caught or explained. New reports keep coming in. Could such creatures possibly exist?

See what you think. This book tells about six legendary beasts. Some may be hoaxes. Some may be real. Some are creatures we know a great deal about, even though we don't believe in them. Some are creatures we know nothing about, but they must be real—we've seen them.

You will hear a lot of stories in your life. Some will be true, some won't be true, and some *might* be true. You can practice sorting out these types of stories by reading about these unbelievable beasts.

Everybody knows what a dragon looks like, right? It looks like a cross between a dinosaur and a snake. It has the wings of a bat, a long snout, and a mouth full of teeth. It has pointed ears, and its body is covered with scales. It can fly. It can also blow fire out its nose.

But how do we know all this? No one has ever seen a dragon. After all, dragons do not exist—do they?

But if dragons do not exist, where do all the stories come from? Many people in history have known about this beast. Most of them have believed it was real. And they didn't hear about it from one another. Dragon stories were told in both ancient China and ancient Europe. In those days China and Europe did not know about each other. How could they have made up the same legendary creature? That

in itself is unbelievable. Can two people in different countries have the same dream?

Here's another strange fact. Many places have few dragon stories or none at all. You don't hear much about dragons in ancient Africa or the Americas. India has no myths about dragons.

Most dragon stories come from a certain part of the world. It is a strip of land that

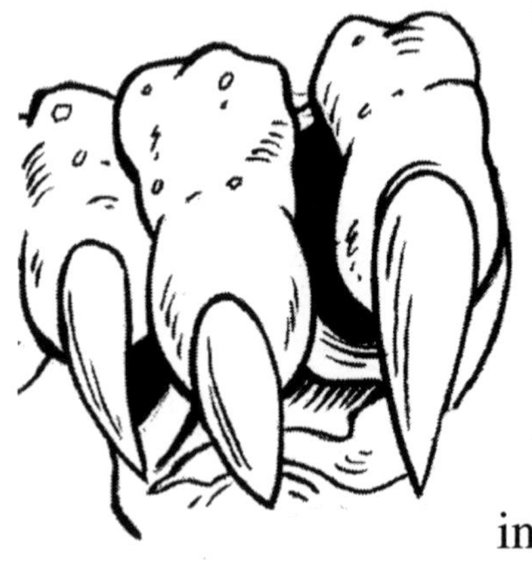

runs from China to England. You might call this the "dragon belt." Why did people in these lands believe in dragons? Could it be that a dragon-like beast really lived there once?

Perhaps the real beast was not exactly like the fairy-tale dragons. Even true stories get puffed up as they are retold. For example, there is the "true" story of the Lambton worm. Surely, over time, a few details have been added to this story. Here is how it goes today.

John Lambton was a young English lord. One Sunday in 1420, he was fishing when he should have been in church. But instead of a fish, he caught a disgusting worm. It had sharp teeth and bad breath. It was covered with slime. Lambton tossed it into a well. He thought the worm was a sign that he should change his way of life. He went off to war.

The worm, however, did not die. It grew into a dragon. It came out of the well all slimy. Its breath was bad enough to kill. It was so big it could wrap itself around a hill nine times. It began to eat cows, sheep, and children. Some brave fellows cut the dragon in half. But both halves lived and grew.

Then there were two monsters.

At last John Lambton came home and killed the dragons. But his family was cursed from then on. They suffered for the next 200 years.

Let's look closely at this story. Which parts are beyond belief? A man fished something from a river that looked like a worm with teeth. This fits an old Chinese legend. They say dragons start out as snakes and live in water for 500 years.

The Lambton worm grew huge and slimy. Is that impossible? Even today the world has some big, slimy worms. In Australia, for example, there is a worm that grows to 10 feet long. It coats itself with slippery slime, which it can squirt 2 feet. If you cut this worm in half, it doesn't die. Both halves keep living and growing.

How is its breath? Don't ask. Does it have teeth? Well, no, but no one says dragons were just worms. John Lambton may have caught some horrid thing we've never seen. It might have looked like a worm when it was young. It might have looked like a lizard once it was fully grown. Maybe it was the last of its kind.

Or maybe not. Even today there is a dragon-like creature in the world called the Komodo dragon. It lives on three small islands in the Indian Ocean. Perhaps it had cousins in the dragon belt long ago.

The Komodo dragon can grow as long as 10 feet. It can weigh up to 300 pounds. It will chase down and eat anything that moves. It can rip a wild pig to pieces with its claws. It has a long, forked, dragon-like tongue.

Storybook dragons live underground. Komodo dragons bury their eggs in deep holes. When the young are born, they dig their way out. What would you think if you saw young Komodo dragons coming out of the ground?

Storybook dragons can fly. Komodo dragons spend their early years in trees. They leap on animals passing below. What would you think if a 10-foot Komodo dragon dropped on you from above?

Storybook dragons are huge. Komodo dragons are only 10 feet long. But their cousins could have been much bigger. And how big would the Komodo dragon look if it was chasing you? Suppose you made it home. How big would it be by the time you were telling your story? Might it have grown to 100 feet by then?

Giants, of course, are real. We have seen them on television. They play for the NBA (National Basketball Association).

But that's not what most people mean by the word "giant." Most people mean a whole different kind of creature.

The Greeks of 2,700 years ago believed in giants. They thought giants were the first living things. The giants they believed in were bigger than the earth. They were bigger than the sky. Those giants gave birth to the gods, who were smaller. And the gods killed the giants and took their place. Later, the gods made even smaller creatures—people.

The Norse believed in giants, too. The Norse lived in northern Europe about 1,200 years ago. The Norse giants and gods were about equal and were always fighting. The Norse thought there would be a final battle someday. It would be gods against giants, head to head. The giants would win, and that would be the end of the world. The Norse had a gloomy view of life.

Later, giants became favorite

characters in fairy tales. These giants were smaller than the Greek and Norse giants. They were not much bigger than redwood trees. They were sort of fat and none too smart. They lived near towns. They were dangerous because they were clumsy. They stepped on farms by accident. They crushed houses. A few of these giants enjoyed eating people. But heroes could always fool them.

Such were the giants of legend. But what about the giants of fact? Did they ever really exist?

It depends on what you mean by "giant."

If you mean really big people, the answer may be yes. Such people may have walked the earth. We do not know for sure, but we have found some clues. There are some really big footprints, for example, in Nevada. They were found on a layer of stone. They are 20 inches long. Compare that to your own feet. And in Wisconsin, a huge stone ax was once found. It was 28 inches wide and weighed 300 pounds. Who could swing an ax like that?

The Delaware Indians have some interesting stories. They say they drove giants out of their lands long ago. The giants fled west, they say. And here is

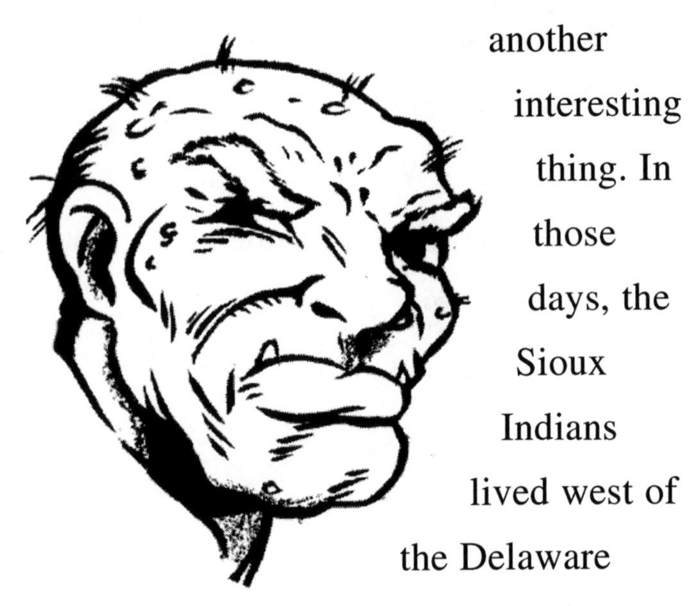

another interesting thing. In those days, the Sioux Indians lived west of the Delaware Indians. They had some legends about giants, too. Their legends say a race of giants once came out of the east.

The two legends fit together perfectly. The Sioux say the giants from the east tried to take their lands, but they fought back. In the end, the Sioux say, they killed all those giants.

There is one more piece to this story. Giant bones have been found in Minnesota. That's where the Sioux lived at the time of their legends. Seven skeletons were found in the woods up there in 1888. Each of those skeletons was about 8 feet tall.

Even today, some people in the world are really tall. In Africa live the Masai people. Masai men often reach heights of 7 feet. Is it such a stretch to think that even taller people once lived on the earth? People who were 8, or 10, or even 15 feet tall?

Here is another reason to think they might have.

A bunch of giant skulls were once found on a small island near Alaska by workers building an airport there. Those skulls were about 22 inches high. (Our skulls measure about 6 to 8 inches top to bottom.) What kind of body went with such a head? It must have been a man or a woman about 20 feet tall. That's taller than a giraffe!

But was it the skull of a human? That's what we don't know. Mistakes are easy to make. The bones of a giant were found in Europe in the 1600s. Experts of the time said they belonged to a 20-foot-tall man. His bones were put in a museum in Paris. There he stayed for almost 200 years. Hundreds of people looked at his bones. The label said he was a German king of times past.

But in the 1800s, experts looked at those bones again. They found that the bones had been put together wrong. When they were put together the right way, everyone had to laugh. They were not the bones of a man after all. They were the bones of a mammoth. That's a kind of elephant.

So we know there were giants long

ago—but they were elephants. And we know there were people long ago—but they were small. We're still waiting for proof that there were ever giant people.

A monster lurks in the ocean. It is huge beyond belief. It has many boneless arms as thick as trees. Each arm has suckers along its whole length. Each arm ends in a claw. Most of the time, this monster feeds on giant sea worms. It catches them with its suckers and pulls them into its beak-like mouth. Then it grinds them to mush and sucks them in like soup.

But sometimes this monster wants a different kind of food. Then it rises with a roar. That's when sailors tremble. No ship on the sea can stand up to the *kraken.*

It sounds like something out of a comic book, doesn't it? The kraken! That's what this snake-armed sea monster was called. Sailors believed in it for thousands of years. They believed the kraken sank ships. It rose from the deep and grabbed ships and crushed them. It wrapped its arms around some ships and yanked them under. Then it ate the drowned sailors down in its dark, wet home.

The heart of the kraken legend was always the kraken's size. Forget about elephants and whales. They were mice and minnows next to the kraken. This was the largest sea monster that ever lived. So said a bishop who lived in the 1600s. He wrote a book about sea monsters. He said the kraken stretched for miles from side to side. When it rose up, it looked like many islands. He had never seen one himself, mind you. He was just passing on what sailors had told him.

If ever a monster sounded fake, it was the kraken. Yet today we know the kraken really exists. But we don't call it the kraken anymore. We now call it the giant squid. It's not as big as the stories said. But it's pretty big. The first one ever found washed up on a beach in 1953. It weighed 29 tons—about 58,000 pounds. It was dead, of course. A live beast of this type has never been caught.

If you leave out size, the giant squid is a perfect kraken. It has a body shaped like a cigar. It has eight powerful arms. It has two tentacles. Each tentacle is lined with suckers that look like saucers. A squid's suckers can stick to almost anything. Each tentacle ends in a catlike claw. The beak of this monster looks like that of a giant parrot. It holds its prey with its arms and tentacles. It then tears at the flesh with its beak.

In 1941, Britain was at war with Germany. A British ship called the *Britannia* was sunk. The sailors tried to escape in lifeboats. Many of the boats turned over, however. Hundreds of people spilled into the sea. One of these sailors was a man named Cox. He said he saw a giant squid pull down the man next to him. Then it pulled down another man. Then another. Suddenly, the end of a tentacle wrapped around his own leg. He pulled free and swam for his life. He made it into a boat, but he was scarred for the rest of his life.

In 1873, two fishermen and a boy fought off an attack by a squid. At least, so they said. They were far from land in a small boat. One of them had his twelve-year-old son, Tom, along. As they rowed along, they saw a clump of seaweed. It had an odd, smooth surface. One of the men poked at it with his oar. Yow! Out of the seaweed came a huge arm. Then came a tentacle. It hit the boat and stuck on. Whap! The men jumped out, but young Tom grabbed an ax. He hacked off the monster's arms. The squid sank in a cloud of black ink.

In 1874, a ship called the *Strathowen* was on the open sea. Far away, its crew saw a ship called the *Pearl.* The people on that ship were fighting with something. The sailors were shooting into the water. Suddenly, huge tentacles rose out of the water and closed around the ship. The *Strathowen* rushed to the rescue but did not get there fast enough. The monster pulled the *Pearl* under. Only five sailors from the *Pearl* lived to tell their story.

Stories like these were quite common long ago. But we don't hear such tales anymore. Today scientists say squid do not attack ships. Perhaps the old stories were not true. After all, the biggest squid we have seen was only about 60 feet long. That's too small to sink a ship.

But there are bigger squid in the ocean. We know this from the scars we have seen on whales. Whales and squid often fight because they like to eat each other. A 60-foot squid has suckers about 4 inches across. But some whales have been caught with sucker scars that came from suckers that were 18 inches across! Those whales, it seems, fought with 300-foot squid. Such squid, if they exist, are the biggest creatures that ever lived!

Long ago there was a city called Troy. A stout wall surrounded the city and kept it safe from enemies. But one morning, the people of Troy—Trojans—saw a huge wooden horse outside their wall. Some of them wanted to bring the horse right into the city. A man named Laocoön, however, spoke fiercely against this idea.

Just as he was talking, a huge snakelike beast came out of the sea. It grabbed Laocoön and his two young sons. It crushed them all and dragged them into the sea. The people of Troy saw this as a clear sign. Laocoön's advice must have been wrong. They brought the horse into their city and had a party. But the horse turned out to be full of Greek soldiers. That night the Greeks came out of the horse and sacked Troy.

The beast that killed Laocoön was a sea serpent. Sailors already knew about this terrible animal. They had seen its kind in the open sea. And sailors have reported seeing such beasts ever since.

Their stories paint a pretty clear picture of the sea serpent. It has the head of a horse and the body of a snake. Yet it also has front and back paws that are like paddles. It swims with an up-and-down, roller-coaster motion. It is long and thick. How long? How thick? That depends on who you ask. It might be as short as 50 feet or as long as 200 feet. The big ones might be 20 feet around.

The sea serpent has humps on its back and quite sharp and frightening teeth. It lives in the ocean, yet it can breathe air. Sometimes it comes ashore to lay eggs. When it does, look out! This serpent will kill anything in its path.

Sailors are not the only ones who have seen sea serpents. Hundreds of people saw one in a city harbor in 1817. The city was Gloucester, Massachusetts. One afternoon a monster reared 8 feet out of the water. It swam toward shore and then turned. As it swam away, people saw humps on its back.

A team of scientists went looking for that beast. They took along a doctor in case someone got hurt. They took along a judge to make sure everybody told the truth, but none of them had anything to tell. They didn't see anything.

While they were gone, however, two boys found a black snake with humps on its back. They thought it might be a baby sea serpent. They sold it to the scientists. After much study, the scientists admitted they had never seen anything like it.

This sea serpent was seen off and on for about 30 years. It was seen up and down the coast of Massachusetts. It was seen by hundreds of people. Surely this creature existed. All those people must have seen *something.* But what did they see? That is the question.

Was it a ribbonfish? Was it some kind of giant eel? We've never seen an eel more than 10 feet long, but does that mean bigger eels don't exist?

Or are sea serpents some kind of dinosaur?

Many sailors' pictures of sea serpents

sure look like dinosaurs. We are told that dinosaurs died out millions of years ago. But perhaps a few types never did die out. Perhaps we don't see them much because they live in the deepest parts of the ocean. You might ask why we never find their bones. But that is no mystery at all. If they live in the water, they sink when they die. Their bones settle into the mud of the ocean floor, where we will never find them.

This idea has not been proved, but is it possible?

Yes, it is. The ocean is huge. We know less about its deepest parts than we know about the moon. At least we can see the moon. We can get a close look at it with telescopes. People have set foot up there.

But people have never set foot on the deepest ocean floor. No one can go down there. The weight of water is too great. This weight is called water pressure. It squeezes you from every side. The deeper you go, the harder it squeezes. A mile down, the water pressure can crush you. And some parts of the ocean are more than 5 miles deep!

You can go some way down into the

ocean in a diving bell. This round steel ball keeps you from getting crushed. But you can't see much out of a diving bell. The windows are too thick, and the ocean is too dark. If you bring a light, it won't shine far in the murky water.

So what lives down there in the deepest ocean? We can only guess.

In 1940, an unbelievable beast turned up in Ithaca, New York. It walked across the Cornell College campus. No one saw it, but they saw its footprints. The tracks appeared one morning after a snowstorm. They were the only tracks to be seen in that fresh snow.

People recognized the animal from its footprints. It was not some weird and unknown creature. It was just a rhinoceros. But what was a rhinoceros doing in New York? On a college campus? That was the unbelievable part. Rhinoceros only live in Africa and Asia. Where had it come from? Where did it go?

The tracks started near some of the main buildings. They ran across some fields, went to the middle of an ice-covered lake, and ended at a hole in the ice.

It was easy to see what had happened. A rhino dropped out of the sky. It walked onto the lake. It fell through the ice and drowned. But where was its body?

Strangely enough, the body of that beast was never found.

Well, actually, this was not so strange. Many years later, the truth came out. A student named Hugh Troy made those tracks. He had a wastebasket that was shaped like a rhinoceros foot. Hugh and a friend filled that wastebasket with metal.

They hung it from a very long rope. Each boy took one end of the rope, and they walked across the campus.

Every few feet they stopped and let the basket down. As it sank into the snow, it made a footprint. Then they pulled the rope tight, and the basket lifted. They walked forward again. In this way, they made the famous rhinoceros tracks of Cornell.

This joke should make us look closely at stories about legendary

creatures. One of the most famous of these beasts is the Loch Ness monster. Loch Ness is a deep lake in Scotland. There has long been a story that some kind of monster lives in this lake. It is supposed to look like a sea serpent. Many people have reported seeing it. None of them, however, could ever prove their claim.

Then in 1934, the so-called "Surgeon's

Photo" was published. Here at last was proof that the Loch Ness monster was real. This picture was taken by R. Kenneth Wilson. He was not some wacky sea serpent nut. He was a well-known, respectable London doctor. His photo showed a creature with a long neck and a small head. People could see pretty clearly what it was—a dinosaur.

But on March 13, 1994, the truth came out about that photo. A London newspaper broke the news. A man named Marmaduke Wetherell faked the photo. His stepson, Christian Spurling, helped him. Dr. R. Kenneth Wilson was in on the joke, too.

Wetherell was a big-game hunter and filmmaker. He wanted to make a film about the Loch Ness monster. He knew he could make more money if the monster was real, so he and his stepson got together to create a monster. They made it out of plastic wood. It was about a foot high. They tied it to a toy submarine. They pushed the toy out into the lake and took a picture of the model. In a picture, something small and close can look like something big and far away. This was how the "Surgeon's Photo" worked. A small model was made to look like a huge serpent. Wetherell and Spurling gave their film to Wilson. He thought it was just a good joke. He brought the film to a photo shop and said the pictures were his.

As soon as the photos were published, the world went wild. Everyone was excited. Wilson was embarrassed. He did not feel he could admit he had played a trick just then. He kept his mouth shut, waiting for the news to die down.

But the excitement never did die. Thousands of people came to the lake to see the monster. The Loch Ness monster became a business. And the longer Wilson kept quiet, the harder it was to tell the truth. So he went to his grave with his secret. So did Wetherell. It was the stepson, Spurling, who finally told the truth. And he was 90 years old by then. He was on his deathbed, in fact.

So today we know the Loch Ness monster is real. We know it lies buried in the mud at Loch Ness. But we also know that it is one foot high and made of plastic.

Mermaids are half fish and half human. People have believed in these creatures for at least 7,000 years. In early times, people carved sculptures of mermaid goddesses. Later, people said mermaids were beautiful spirits who made sailors drown. Then people said mermaids were lovely animals of some kind. But they never stopped believing in mermaids.

Christopher Columbus saw three mermaids in America. He was not surprised. He expected such sights in this strange new world.

So did the explorer Henry Hudson. He saw a mermaid in 1608 off the coast of Canada. He was very matter-of-fact about it. "This morning, saw a mermaid," he wrote in his notebook. He went on to tell how his sailors crowded to the railing to see her. The mermaid looked back. She had the tail and fins of a fish. From the belly up, however, she was shaped like a woman. Suddenly she dove into the water and vanished.

Another explorer who saw a mermaid was Captain Richard Whitbourne. He mentioned how beautiful this mermaid was. Her hair was black with streaks of blue, he said. She came right up to the ship. Then, one of his sailors "clobbered" the poor thing with an oar.

Perhaps the sailor was scared. By this time, some frightening stories were being told about mermaids. Some sailors said they grabbed humans in the water and squeezed them to death. They let out sad sighs while they were doing this. But they got over their sadness. Once their victim was dead, they carried him to some underwater cave and ate him. They did not just gobble him up, however. The mermaids were polite. They ate only selected bits of him. They nibbled on ears and eyes. They also ate fingers and toes.

As the years passed, more and more sailors claimed they had seen mermaids. No one wanted to be left out. The creatures they described grew ever more beautiful. Some sailors started showing "mermaid mummies" at carnivals. They made these "mermaids" out of old bones, monkey parts, and dried fish skins. Many people paid good money to see these fakes. They were fooled because they wanted so much to believe in mermaids.

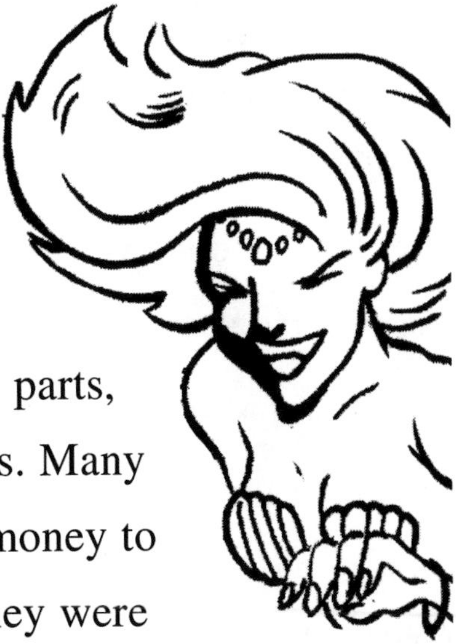

In 1842, one old sea captain had what he called the "Famous Feejee Mermaid." He was trying to get people on the street to pay for a glimpse of it, but most people said, "Go away and take your smelly mermaid with you."

Then he met P. T. Barnum, the showman. Barnum ran a circus. When he saw the "Feejee Mermaid," he smelled money. He secretly bought the mermaid.

Then he wrote a letter to the papers under a fake name. He complained about a man named Dr. Griffin. He said this Dr. Griffin had a mermaid mummy, but he wouldn't show it to anyone in America. He was going to take it to England.

The next day many people wrote angry letters to the newspaper. They said Americans should have a chance to see the mermaid, too. Griffin wrote to the papers and said no. He would never let Americans see his mermaid. One day Dr. Griffin bumped into P. T. Barnum in a public place. Barnum loudly demanded to buy the mermaid. Griffin loudly said no. Their argument became big news. The whole city took sides. Anger against Dr. Griffin kept building up.

Of course, Dr. Griffin was not really a doctor. And his name was not Griffin. He worked for Barnum. When the anger was at its height, he gave in. He agreed to "let" Barnum show the mermaid for one week only. In that week, Barnum made many thousands of dollars. Then he cheerfully admitted he had tricked the

public. He told the newspapers he owned the mermaid. He moved it to his museum across the street, and there it stayed. Was he ashamed of himself? Not at all. "There's a sucker born every minute," he said, "and I was born to take his money."

Today, scientists think they know what Columbus and the others saw. Those were not mermaids but manatees. A manatee is also called a sea cow. These harmless beasts do little but move slowly through the water, eating seaweed. Their skin is gray, but tiny, colorful plants grow on them. These can look like makeup and jewelry. Seaweed hanging on them can look like hair. The manatee's nose looks sort of human. Its flippers can look like arms. It has fingers and even fingernails.

Of course, mermaids are supposed to be beautiful. A manatee is not beautiful, except to another manatee. It has ragged fur and a big mustache. It has big, fat split lips. Its eyes are sunk in deep rolls of fat. Its nose is huge and thick. No wonder Columbus was disappointed in the mermaids he saw. "They are not as beautiful as they are painted," he wrote.

So there you have the sad story of the mermaid. She started out as a goddess. She ended up as a sea cow.